BIZARRE DINOSAURS

BIZARRE

Can you find this bizarre dinosaur in the book? (For answer, see page 32.)

DINOSAURS

SOME VERY STRANGE CREATURES AND WHY WE THINK THEY GOT THAT WAY

CHRISTOPHER SLOAN

WITH A FOREWORD BY **JAMES CLARK** AND **CATHY FORSTER**

NATIONAL GEOGRAPHIC
WASHINGTON, D.C.

To all the National Geographic staff, at the magazine, in television, and in other divisions, as well as to the many talented artists and scientists who helped bring these dinosaurs to life. —CS

Founded in 1888, the National Geographic Society is one of the largest nonprofit scientific and educational organizations in the world. It reaches more than 285 million people worldwide each month through its official journal, NATIONAL GEOGRAPHIC, and its four other magazines; the National Geographic Channel; television documentaries; radio programs; films; books; videos and DVDs; maps; and interactive media. National Geographic has funded more than 8,000 scientific research projects and supports an education program combating geographic illiteracy.

For more information, please call
1-800-NGS LINE (647-5463) or write to the following address:
NATIONAL GEOGRAPHIC SOCIETY
1145 17th Street N.W., Washington, D.C. 20036-4688 U.S.A.

Visit us online at www.nationalgeographic.com/books
Librarians and teachers, visit us at www.ngchildrensbooks.org

For information about special discounts for bulk purchases, please contact
National Geographic Books Special Sales: ngspecsales@ngs.org.

For rights or permissions inquiries, please contact
National Geographic Books Subsidiary Rights: ngbookrights@ngs.org.

Library of Congress Cataloging-in-Publication Data available from the publisher on request.
Trade Hardcover ISBN 978-1-4263-0330-2
Reinforced Library Edition ISBN 978-1-4263-0331-9
Scholastic Edition ISBN 978-1-4263-0647-1

Printed in China

09/RRDS/1

TABLE OF CONTENTS

This room is chock-a-block with fossils from our expeditions with Chinese scientists to western China. Careful study of these fossils will give us a better picture of the world of dinosaurs.

DINOSAURS SEEM LIKE SOMETHING from a fantasy world, but unlike unicorns, gryphons, and dragons, they actually existed. We know of them mostly from their bones, and there is nothing so exciting as watching the bones of a new dinosaur slowly take shape as they are extracted from their rocky grave. Paleontologists like us spend much of our lives digging for new fossils and then studying them to decipher the stories they hold. When a fossil is being excavated, our minds are racing: What kind of dinosaur is it? How much is preserved? Are there clues to how it died, what it ate, and how it moved? It is like assembling a jigsaw puzzle missing most of the pieces, and it's not always easy to see the whole picture. In this book you will find some surprising and baffling discoveries, dinosaurs with features nobody fully understands. We may never know everything we would like to know about them, but we can marvel at their strangeness. And who knows, perhaps one day you will grow up to be a paleontologist and discover even more bizarre dinosaurs. Or you might be the one to finally understand how some of their odd features were used.

—JAMES CLARK and CATHY FORSTER

NAME
AMARGASAURUS
(UH-MAR-GUH-SAWR-US)

YEAR NAMED
1991

TYPE OF DINOSAUR
SAUROPOD

NORMAL ADULT SIZE
33 FEET

STOMPING GROUND
PATAGONIA, ARGENTINA,
SOUTH AMERICA

WHEN IT LIVED
130 TO 125 MILLION
YEARS AGO

ON THE MENU
PLANTS

Amargasaurus's closest relative
lived in what is now East Africa,
but it didn't share its strange
back fringe.

AMARGASAURUS
HAD A FRINGED BACK.

SEA MONSTERS with fishlike fins on their backs come to mind when we try to imagine what *Amargasaurus* looked like. One finlike row would be bizarre enough, but the double row of spikes strung along *Amargasaurus's* back pushes it to extremes. Why the fringe? It would have been useless for defense, but it could have been attractive to mates. But maybe we're interpreting the spines incorrectly. Perhaps instead of a double fringe, the two rows of back spines supported a mass of flesh. A thick, deep neck might have helped protect *Amargasaurus* by making the animal look too big for some predators to eat.

Scientists discovered a fairly complete skeleton of *Amargasaurus* in Argentina.

9

CARNOTAURUS
HAD BULL HORNS.

CARNOTAURUS was a distant relative of *Tyrannosaurus rex,* and its tiny arms give it a *T. rex* look. Yet *Carnotaurus* had small teeth for a big meat-eating hunter. It also had a pair of stubby, chunky horns jutting out from its brow like a bull. Brow horns like these are mostly seen among ceratopsids—plant-eating dinosaurs, not meat-eaters. Ceratopsids may have used their horns for defense, for competing with rivals, or for attracting mates. It is possible that *Carnotaurus* was a scavenger, rather than a big hunter, and used its horns in the same ways, but between meaty meals.

Carnotaurus's name, meaning "meat-bull," links its bull-like horns to its meat-eating habits.

10

The almost complete fossil of *Carnotaurus* had horns and skin impressions that showed it had bumps along its back.

NAME
CARNOTAURUS
(KAR-NO-TAWR-US)

YEAR NAMED
1985

TYPE OF DINOSAUR
THEROPOD

NORMAL ADULT SIZE
30 FEET

STOMPING GROUND
PATAGONIA, ARGENTINA, SOUTH AMERICA

WHEN IT LIVED
83 to 65 MILLION YEARS AGO

ON THE MENU
MEAT

11

Stegosaurs such as *Tuojiangosaurus* had many styles of armor. But their body shape was almost always the same, a small head with a tanklike body.

EXPERT KNOWLEDGE

NAME
TUOJIANGOSAURUS
(TWHOA-JEE-ANG-OH-SAWR-US)
. . . .
YEAR NAMED
1977
. . . .
TYPE OF DINOSAUR
STEGOSAUR
. . . .
NORMAL ADULT SIZE
23 FEET
. . . .
STOMPING GROUND
SICHUAN, CHINA, ASIA
. . . .
WHEN IT LIVED
161 to 155 MILLION
YEARS AGO
. . . .
ON THE MENU
PLANTS

TUOJIANGOSAURUS
HAD SPIKED SHOULDERS.

MANY STEGOSAURS have fierce-looking tail spikes and what look like flat stones sticking out of their backs. These are fancy forms of osteoderms, bony plates that some animals, such as dinosaurs and crocodiles, wear in their skin. *Tuojiangosaurus* added one more weapon to its armor—shoulder spikes that jut out from its shoulders. It is possible that all of this scary gear was only used to look impressive to mates, but it must also have made *Tuojiangosaurus* look a little less tasty to predators.

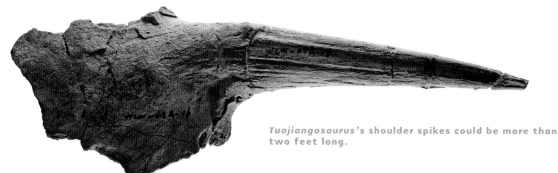

Tuojiangosaurus's shoulder spikes could be more than two feet long.

13

NIGERSAURUS

HAD A VERY WIDE MOUTH.

NO OTHER ANIMAL—EXTINCT OR ALIVE—HAS A MUZZLE quite like *Nigersaurus.* Other long-necked sauropods had narrow snouts with peglike teeth, nothing like *Nigersaurus*'s wide mouth with comblike rows of tiny teeth. Behind each toothy row in *Nigersaurus*'s skull sit as many as eight other sets of teeth—that's around 500 spare teeth standing ready to replace worn ones. *Nigersaurus* held its head at a sharp angle to its neck, causing its mouth to be pointed toward the ground. This dinosaur was found in the Sahara desert, which in its time was a wet, plant-rich environment. Its unusual mouth was probably useful for constantly mowing soft plants.

Nigersaurus's thin skull bones lead scientists to think it may not have been able to eat much more than soft plants.

Many fossils of medium-sized *Nigersaurus* have been found in Niger. Its name means "Niger lizard."

NAME
NIGERSAURUS
(NEE-ZHERE-SAWR-US)

YEAR NAMED
1999

TYPE OF DINOSAUR
SAUROPOD

NORMAL ADULT SIZE
30 FEET

STOMPING GROUND
SAHARA DESERT, NIGER,
AFRICA

WHEN IT LIVED
110 MILLION
YEARS AGO

ON THE MENU
PLANTS

Masiakasaurus looked very fierce, but it had to watch out for the larger meat-eating dinosaurs and the many kinds of crocodiles living around it in Madagascar.

EXPERT KNOWLEDGE

NAME
MASIAKASAURUS
(MUH-SHEE-KUH-SAWR-US)

YEAR NAMED
2001

TYPE OF DINOSAUR
THEROPOD

NORMAL ADULT SIZE
7 FEET

STOMPING GROUND
MAHAJUNGA, MADAGASCAR, AFRICA

WHEN IT LIVED
70 TO 65 MILLION YEARS AGO

ON THE MENU
MEAT

MASIAKASAURUS
HAD A NASTY BITE.

THE CHAMPION OF BIZARRE TEETH is *Masiakasaurus*, meaning "vicious lizard." This collie-sized dinosaur from Madagascar was a meat-eater, but exactly how it hunted we don't know because no living animal has teeth like this. In the back of its mouth, *Masiakasaurus's* teeth were shaped like knives with serrated edges, but toward the front they were cone-shaped, curved, and pointed nearly straight ahead. Knifelike teeth are good for slicing, so maybe *Masiakasaurus* opened its mouth wide and sliced larger prey with its back teeth. The hooked front teeth may have been used for stabbing or snagging small mammals, lizards, or birds.

The front part of *Masiakasaurus's* lower jaw shows a couple of curved teeth.

17

Deinocheirus's long arms may have been attached to a 40-foot body.

DEINOCHEIRUS
HAD LONG, CLAWED ARMS.

IF EVER THERE WAS A DINOSAUR MYSTERY, it is Mongolia's *Deinocheirus,* meaning "terrible hand." Only its arms and a few other bits have ever been found. But what arms! Each one is eight feet long with three ten-inch claws at the end. No one really knows what *Deinocheirus* was. Perhaps it had the long neck, legs, and tail of an ornithomimosaur, and its plant-eating habits as well. But to work with these arms, its body would have been enormous, as big as a *T. rex.*

EXPERT KNOWLEDGE

NAME
DEINOCHEIRUS
(DYE-NO-KAI-RUS)

YEAR NAMED
1970

TYPE OF DINOSAUR
THEROPOD

NORMAL ADULT SIZE
UP TO 40 FEET

STOMPING GROUND
GOBI DESERT OF MONGOLIA,
ASIA

WHEN IT LIVED
70 MILLION
YEARS AGO

ON THE MENU
PROBABLY PLANTS

Nobody knows how feathery
Deinocheirus might have been.
Large dinosaurs would have had
fewer feathers than small ones
because larger animals need to
lose body heat, not keep it.

Dracorex was a pachycephalosaur, meaning "thick-headed lizard."

EXPERT KNOWLEDGE

NAME
**DRACOREX
(DRA-KOHR-EX)**

YEAR NAMED
2006

TYPE OF DINOSAUR
PACHYCEPHALOSAUR

NORMAL ADULT SIZE
10 FEET

STOMPING GROUND
**SOUTH DAKOTA, U.S.A.,
NORTH AMERICA**

WHEN IT LIVED
**67 to 65 MILLION
YEARS AGO**

ON THE MENU
PLANTS

DRACOREX
HAD A VERY BUMPY HEAD.

THE SPIKY SKULL OF THIS DINOSAUR is so nasty looking it was named *Dracorex hogwartsia,* meaning "dragon king of Hogwarts," for the wizardry school of the Harry Potter books. But this creature was not as fierce as it appears. It is a plant-eating pachycephalosaur. Others of this group sport helmetlike bony domes on their heads. It may be that they used their thick skulls to butt each other, the way rams and goats do today. Some scientists think *Dracorex* isn't a separate creature at all, but a young pachycephalosaur that hasn't grown its dome yet.

This fossil skull of *Dracorex* was found in the famous fossil formation known as Hell Creek, in South Dakota.

21

PARASAUROLOPHUS
HAD A MUSICAL HEAD.

PARASAUROLOPHUS HAD THE MOST BIZARRE HEADGEAR of any of the duckbill dinosaurs—and the most puzzling. When *Parasaurolophus* breathed through its nose, air would pass through a doubled-back tube inside the long crest. Was it for a super sense of smell? To warm the air? Just for show? Scientists made a model to see what sound the tube would make if air passed through it. They discovered that *Parasaurolophus's* crest could make wonderful hornlike sounds. It may have used these sounds to communicate with others.

22

These duckbilled hadrosaurs are known for their bill-like mouth and crest, but the inside of their mouth is bizarre as well. They have thousands of teeth.

NAME
PARASAUROLOPHUS
(PARE-UH-SAWR-*ALL*-UH-FUSS)

YEAR NAMED
1922

TYPE OF DINOSAUR
HADROSAUR

NORMAL ADULT SIZE
31 FEET

STOMPING GROUND
ALBERTA, CANADA, AND NEW MEXICO, U.S.A., NORTH AMERICA

WHEN IT LIVED
76 MILLION YEARS AGO

ON THE MENU
PLANTS

EXPERT KNOWLEDGE

NAME
STYRACOSAURUS
(STY-RACK-OH-SAWR-US)

YEAR NAMED
1913

TYPE OF DINOSAUR
CERATOPSID

NORMAL ADULT SIZE
18 FEET

STOMPING GROUND
ALBERTA, CANADA,
NORTH AMERICA

WHEN IT LIVED
75 MILLION
YEARS AGO

ON THE MENU
PLANTS

Horned dinosaurs with frills
appear to have got their start
in Asia, but most of the large
ones with elaborate head
armor, such as *Styraco-
saurus*, have been found in
North America.

STYRACOSAURUS
HAD A HUGE SPIKED COLLAR.

THE SHARP SPIKES on *Styracosaurus's* neck frill look dangerous, but these animals weren't predators. And the spikes probably added no more protection than the less-spiky frills of other ceratopsid dinosaurs. A large meat-eater, such as *Albertosaurus,* could easily have chomped on *Styracosaurus's* unprotected hindquarters. It may be that the main purpose of the armor was not offense *or* defense. It is just as likely that the big frills were used to show off and attract mates. The earliest known member of this group, *Yinlong,* was found in 2004 in western China. Knobs on the back of its skull show that horned dinosaurs were close relatives of the pachycephalosaurs.

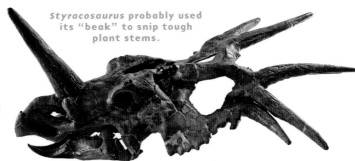

Styracosaurus probably used its "beak" to snip tough plant stems.

25

EPIDENDROSAURUS
HAD A SUPER-LONG FINGER.

THE AYE-AYE, a bizarre lemur from Madagascar, has one extra-long finger on each hand that it uses to fish tasty bugs out of holes in tree bark. That

LONG THIRD FINGER →

← HIND FOOT

Epidendrosaurus's long finger was preserved as an impression on this flat stone.

may be what tiny *Epidendrosaurus* was doing with its super-long finger as well. Its sharp, curved claws also suggest that this Chinese dinosaur, like the aye-aye, scampered around in trees. A close relative of the earliest birds, *Epidendrosaurus* was likely covered in a feathery coat. Yet unlike *Microraptor*, another tiny, feathered theropod, there is no evidence *Epidendrosaurus* flew.

NAME
EPIDENDROSAURUS
(EHP-IH-DEN-DROH-SAWR-US)

YEAR NAMED
2002

TYPE OF DINOSAUR
THEROPOD

NORMAL ADULT SIZE
LESS THAN ONE FOOT

STOMPING GROUND
GOBI DESERT OF CHINA, ASIA

WHEN IT LIVED
160 MILLION
YEARS AGO

ON THE MENU
SMALL MAMMALS, INSECTS

Epidendrosaurus's third finger is almost twice as long
as its other fingers.

27

EXPERT KNOWLEDGE

NAME
GIGANTORAPTOR
(JAI-GAN-TOH-RAP-TUR)

YEAR NAMED
2007

TYPE OF DINOSAUR
THEROPOD

NORMAL ADULT SIZE
26 FEET

STOMPING GROUND
GOBI DESERT OF CHINA, ASIA

WHEN IT LIVED
85 MILLION
YEARS AGO

ON THE MENU
PROBABLY MEAT

Other fossilized oviraptorids have been found
sitting on clutches of eggs like nesting birds.
It is possible that *Gigantoraptor* did the same.

GIGANTORAPTOR
HAD A GIANT BEAK.

NO ONE EXPECTED ANYTHING LIKE GIGANTORAPTOR, a giant birdlike dinosaur, to ever be found. Yet that's what happened in 2005. Weighing in at an estimated 3,000 pounds, *Gigantoraptor* is many times bigger than other oviraptorids, which are the size of ostriches or smaller. What surprised scientists most is that they thought dinosaurs became smaller as they became more birdlike. But *Gigantoraptor* upsets that idea. This dinosaur was probably a meat-eater like other theropods, but it is possible that it ate plants as its much smaller cousin *Caudipteryx* did. *Gigantoraptor* might have had feathers like *Caudipteryx*, too, but how feathery it was, no one knows. It probably looked like a giant parrot with a bony tail, with at least some feathers and a big toothless beak.

PARALITITAN was among the largest of the sauropods. It weighed at least 40 tons, about the same as eight pickup trucks.

SPINOSAURUS is best known for the six-foot-long spines that may have made a sail or a hump on its back.

AFROVENATOR, whose name means "African hunter," may have been a distant relative of *Spinosaurus*.

CARCHARODONTOSAURUS Named "shark-toothed dinosaur," *Carcharodontosaurus* was among the largest known meat-eaters.

NIGERSAURUS

MAJUNGASAURUS was the biggest meat-eater in Madagascar, which broke off from Gondwana and grew its own dinosaurs for millions of years.

AMARGASAURUS

MASIAKASAURUS

LEAELLYNASAURA was from the very far south of Gondwana. It might have had eyes that could see well during cold, dark winter months.

CARNOTAURUS

GONDWANA
THE SOUTHERN HEMISPHERE

BIZARRE DINOSAURS didn't live alone. They lived with many other dinosaurs, as well as other animals and plenty of plants. They lived in many places around the world, over millions of years. For much of the time dinosaurs ruled the Earth, there were only two continents. These continents were so big we call them supercontinents. The one in the southern hemisphere is called Gondwana. On this page is a selection of typical Gondwanan dinosaurs, a mix of some of the dinosaurs you met earlier in the book and some others you might already know.

TYRANNOSAURUS REX was a giant once thought to have the biggest head among meat-eaters. That award now goes to a dinosaur from Gondwana, *Giganotosaurus*.

MAMENCHISAURUS had a 36-foot-long neck, one of the longest known among dinosaurs.

PARASAUROLOPHUS

ERKETU, found in Mongolia, had an extremely long neck for its size.

GIGANTORAPTOR

TUOJIANGOSAURUS

VELOCIRAPTOR was a close relative of birds. It had long arms that could reach out and quickly grab prey, as well as a large slashing claw on each foot.

STYRACOSAURUS

SINOSAUROPTERYX caught the world by surprise in 1996 when it was found fossilized with downlike feathers preserved along its back and on its head.

MONONYKUS had a single large claw for a hand. Maybe it used it for digging up insects.

LAURASIA
THE NORTHERN HEMISPHERE

THE SUPERCONTINENT of Laurasia was separated from Gondwana long enough for the dinosaurs in the two hemispheres to become quite different. On this page is a group of Laurasian dinosaurs, again a mix of those you met earlier and some you might know already. By the end of the Mesozoic era (dinosaur times), sauropods such as *Paralititan* were the main plant-eaters in Gondwana, while in Laurasia it was dinosaurs like *Styracosaurus* and *Parasaurolophus*. The meat-eaters in Gondwana were mostly abelisaurs such as *Carnotaurus*, and those in Laurasia were coelurosaurs such as *T. rex*.

GLOSSARY

ABELISAUR: A group of meat-eaters that lived mostly on the Southern Hemisphere supercontinent of Gondwana.

CERATOPSID: One of five groups of bird-hipped, or ornithischian, dinosaurs. Ceratopsids walked on all fours and had horns and elaborate bony frills.

CAUDIPTERYX: A small Chinese beaked theropod found fossilized with small stones in its gut to help it digest plants.

COELUROSAUR: A member of Coelurosauria, a group of theropods closely related to, and including, birds.

HADROSAUR: A member of a group of bird-hipped, or ornithischian, dinosaurs. Hadrosaurs walked on four legs much of the time, had bill-like mouths, and are called "duckbills."

MESOZOIC: A geological era that lasted from 251 to 65 million years ago. It is often called the Age of Dinosaurs since they were the dominant land animal of that time. It is broken into three main periods, the Triassic (251 to 199 million years ago), the Jurassic (199 to 145 million years ago), and the Cretaceous (145 to 65 million years ago).

ORNITHOMIMOSAUR: A group of theropods, most of which were toothless and had horny beaks. Their appearance was ostrich-like, earning them their name, which means "bird-mimic lizard."

OVIRAPTORID: A birdlike theropod with a shortened snout and a beaklike, toothless mouth.

PACHYCEPHALOSAUR: A member of Pachycephalosauria, one of five groups of bird-hipped, or ornithischian, dinosaurs. They walked on two legs and had large bony domes on their skulls.

PREDATOR: An animal that lives by preying on others.

SAUROPOD: A member of Sauropoda, one of the two main branches of the lizard-hipped, or saurischian, dinosaurs. They walked on four legs and had long necks and large bodies.

SCAVENGER: An animal that feeds on animals that are already dead.

STEGOSAUR: A member of Stegosauria, one of five groups of bird-hipped, or ornithischian, dinosaurs. Stegosaurs walked on four legs and had small heads and large tank-like bodies with armored plates and spikes.

THEROPOD: A member of Theropoda, one of the two main branches of the lizard-hipped, or saurischian dinosaurs. They had three toes, walked upright on two legs, and most were meat-eaters.

CREDITS

The realistic color illustrations in this book are computer-generated models that took many people to create. The project was led by the Art Department at National Geographic Magazine. The base models for all of the dinosaurs were prepared by 422 South. All of the photography is by Ira Block, unless otherwise noted.
Amargasaurus: Art by Renegade 9. Photographed at Museo Argentino de Ciencias Naturales (MACN), Buenos Aires.
Carnotaurus: Art by Pixeldust Studios. Photographed at MACN.
Tuojiangosaurus: Art By Pixeldust Studios. Photographed at the Institute of Vertebrate Paleontology and Paleoanthropology (IVPP), Beijing.
Nigersaurus: Art by Pixeldust studios. Photo © M. Hettwer, courtesy of Project Exploration.
Masiakasaurus: Art by Pixeldust Studios. Fossil from the collection of the Université d'Antananarivo, Madagascar.
Deinocheirus: Art by Pixeldust Studios. Fossil from the collection of the Mongolian Academy of Sciences.
Dracorex: Art by DamnFX. Photographed at the Children's Museum of Indianapolis.
Parasaurolophus: Art by Pixeldust Studios. Photograph taken at the Royal Ontario Museum (ROM), Toronto.
Styracosaurus: Art by Renegade 9. Photographed at ROM, Toronto.
Epidendrosaurus: Art by Pixeldust Studios. Photographed at IVPP, Beijing.
Gigantoraptor: Art by Pixeldust Studios.
Pages 30-31: Art by Pixeldust Studios.

Answer to question on title page: Tuojiangosaurus